30 POEMS IN 30 DAYS:
POETRY PROMPTS INSPIRED BY
TRIO HOUSE PRESS POETS

Trio House Press
1st edition

ISBN: 978-1-949487-31-2

Interior design by Molly Kanach
Cover art by Jeffrey Scherer
Cover design by Molly Kanach
Editing by Kris Bigalk and Lisa Ronan

Trio House Press
Minneapolis, MN
www.triohousepress.org

30 Poems in 30 Days:
Poetry Prompts Inspired by *Trio House Press* Poets

Table of Contents

Sunshine O'Donnell
from *States of Arousal* (2023)

North Philly in August

Scattered parasol branches, their
canopies shielding
blunt ends and bottles, how the
shards of glass glitter
by a curb that crumbles like cake.

The Ladies in Hats are still ladies and all
the boys bow, cussing suspended
till the Ladies sail past. The heat makes thick
their regality. The brave
stockinged legs and canes carefully
navigate the gutted path.

The Ladies do not sweat,
but the boys do. They peel off
giant white t-shirts and play, become
master hunters of shade. The walls
engorge with drowsy whorls
from old leaks and paint, the hot
bricks broken and ribbons
of paper that uncling
and curl, dipping
down past the coke vines and the heeled shoes, down past
the sacred procession, then down where elaborate
shadows have seeped
into the ground like oil.

Prompt:
Write a poem starting from a title that includes your current town or city and
the month. In the poem describe a scene as a detached observer, much like
Sunshine O'Donnell does in this poem, evoking unique details of that town or
city, especially those unique to the month or season.

Steven Riel
from *Fellow Odd Fellow* (2013)

Cyndi Lauper

From the first bash of drums,
        we can bet this won't be pretty.
She's dialing up 911--
        in a stomp-squeal frenzy of escape.
a wail all lisp & ache, its silver spike
        heels nearly skewering comic-book scraps,
untied ribbons underfoot.

        A soul's entrails. Road-kill of an ecstasy
that never looked both ways.
        Skipped drumbeats ricochet
down the block. An empty lot.
        Her siren's stiletto
stab-stiches the sky.
        A house of cards
props up one final offer
        till our blond stops holding her
breath.

        Girl-wire whose plea
scrapes down to grieving
        baby talk. The beauty is we know
what she's groaning about.

Prompt:
Write a poem about a well-known performer you admire, or one you find
comes to mind often. Like Riel, use language, images, and metaphors to evoke
the performer's style of vocalization, movement, or other element of their
performances that make them unique. Experiment with line syllables and length.

Sandy Longhorn
from *The Alchemy of My Mortal Form* (2015)

I Have Gone Shimmering Into Ungentle Sleep

This fever is my tutor. It lectures
scarlet on my cheeks, pale quarter-moons

on all my fingernails, a heart that gallops beneath
the cold sting of stethoscpes unleashed.

I repose & ripen with the weight of secrets,
for I swore an oath to silence.

This bed my penitentiary, though
my chains pointless, cotton-woven.

Lethargy of limbs another symptom
pressed into the chart. The noise of the pen

blisters the brain. The catheter in the vein
delivers ruination, dreams induced to knock

my damaged crown askew. When I wake, my bones
have been replaced with porcelain, sinew

altered to wire, & my tongue, my tongue
lets loose what once was barred & guarded.

Prompt:
Write a poem about symptoms of an illness you have experienced or are
experiencing, using the couplet form. Experiment with enjambing lines between
stanzas to add tension or interest to the poem.

Tara Betts
from *Break the Habit* (2016)

A First Kiss

She is thirty-eight, and drugstore attempts
to conceal whitened temples and icy roots
still work for almost three weeks. Returning
home to her ex-husband's emptied drawers
reminds her how far the first kiss was, not
her husband, but with a man who ties her
to childhood with a ribbon of his sweet.

Twenty-five years ago pretends
to take the time that one star travels
to naked eyes on earth. The first man
to kiss her after her husband leaves
is an electrical socket, a canyon of blue
sparks, strobe lights, fire trucks, ambulance,
a megaphone, lips fused into circuit.

This spark, not obsolete memory, supposed
extinct species, resuscitates her bold thirteen-
year-old aflutter gasps inside again. She
justifies discarding all kisses found before.

Prompt:
Like Betts, write a poem not about the first time that you did something
momentous (like a first kiss) but the first time you did something after a very
long hiatus -- perhaps when you did something you thought you would never
have a "first" of again. Try using third person, as Betts does, instead of the first-
person point of view.

Kirk Wilson
from *Songbox* (2021)

Rules for Objects

Always say Thank you to the car
after even an unpleasant ride

To the toilet named Magnolia
Good morning

For the terrifying pencil
the telephone you couldn't love
repeatedly
I'm sorry

Carry one another heavily

Be friends

Following the funeral
of the trousers
be lost in grief for days

Prompt:
Make a list of everyday objects and, like Wilson, create a poem made up of
arbitrary rules for how to behave and speak to these objects. Experiment with
short lines and spare prose to add to the irony or humor of the poem.

Jessica Hincapie
from *Bloomer* (2022)

On the One Hand [In the Other]

It seems that the people in my life have become too real
to write about, making poetry a suitable space only for strangers.

The woman at the cemetery, missed by seconds. Her lipstick
kisses still fresh on the marble grave next to Papito's.

There was a girl met in group therapy, whose dealer,
named Temple, blesses every batch of mushrooms she sells.

These days, my houseguests are always at odds with my house
ghosts. The stairwell constantly littered with tin cans

and lynched cats. Obvious death threats, but from
the guests or the ghosts, I have yet to determine.

I've folded these phantoms into talismans time and time again.
Still each year presents itself like a small tight coin.

A fountain of fish I've mistaken for silver. This life
will ask you more than once to make the choice

between starfish or worm. One animal growing back
what was lost, the other learning to live without.

Prompt:
We often write about or to people we know, but what about the chance
encounters or observations we make about strangers? Write a poem that
features these descriptions of strangers you have observed or heard about from
friends. Why did they stick with you, or why did they come to mind? If no reason
seems to be apparent, make one up.

Issam Zineh
from *Unceded Land* (2022)

Citrine
(excerpt)

When I was 8 or 9, my prized possession was a 4 x 6
piece of cardboard with rocks and gemstones glued to it.

I'd carry it in my backpack every day, memorize
the scientific and popular names of each specimen.

I loved how everything had 2 names.
Now you can buy your kids collections

of pre-historic shark teeth and meteorite fragments.
They come with detailed learning guides.

I never thanked you for the citrine you sent
to the house. The handwritten note was lovely.

I didn't understand what you meant at the time
but now it's different. When you wrote just a little something,

I think you meant: When I cry, I don't cry for the inevitable loss.
When you wrote good luck, I think you meant: I hope you open

your eyes and find yourself under a tree laden with fruit
you cannot name. I imagine you outliving me.

My daughter is now the age I was then.
She passes that citrine all gold and white

through her hands. When she asks where I got it--
sometimes I say I found it. Sometimes, I say I bought it a long time ago.

Prompt:
Center a poem on a prized possession you had as a child - maybe, like Zineh, you
received it as a gift, or maybe you bought it yourself - describe the possession
and its context in your life. End the poem with a mystery, as Zineh does - why
does the speaker in the poem lie about the origin of the object? Leave it open.

Annmarie O'Connell
from *Your Immaculate Heart* (2016)

The Angels on Their Porches

The angel elbows on the spiny rails
The angels sitting in a pillow of smoke
The angels lying on one another in the light
The angels spit out by a gust of wind
The angels falling into the past
The angels chewing on the wet black of the earth
The heavy rumble of angels
wading through the pink blossoms
the heavy rumble of dreams
inside angels

Prompt:
Choose a religious or mythological being, like an angel, a demon, a god, or
goddess, and write a list poem in the style of O'Connell, beginning each line with
the same phrase - then switching to a different phrase for the final two lines.

Megan Neville
from *The Fallow*

Objects in the Road Mistaken for Animals

last Friday, a fast food sleeve hurled
from a car, mid-fall, a crooked branch
            of crisp curled leaves, come spring
a bit of frayed rag, formerly blue.
every mile a wind-animated
grocery bag,   steer into the ditch.
            into oncoming traffic, off the bridge.
I swear I sensed its breath --
            it could have been alive.
                        it could have been alive.

Prompt:
Often, we misidentify objects, words, motivations -- write a poem about a time
(or several times) when you did this. Like Neville, avoid using capital letters,
and try enjambing lines to draw attention to important words, or to create the
disconnect between perception and reality.

David Groff
from *Clay* (2012)

Fancy Meeting You Here

You were supposed to be dead,
being missed for so long,
like the others another empty window
in a building blinking out. But there
you were in the Haagen-Daz store,
seamed and thinned but
eating frozen yogurt, unlike a ghost.

Not that you and I had many minutes
remaining on our parking meter.
Your voice as still gut-deep
but full of nothing: lady gurus,
affirmations that kept you alive
(though they missed their shot
with the pessimistic dead...).

A dime of time and the red flag
flipped to the LED zeros
of your lovely eyes. You gave me
a dismissing kiss and ambled out
alive and now less precious
to the street of unmissing persons,
licking your globe of cone.

Prompt:
Write a poem about an unexpected encounter with someone from your past -
either one that really happened, or one that you imagine could happen. Include
details of the encounter, but also your own inner dialogue, as Groff does.

John W Evans
from *The Consolations* (2013)

Baby Ducks

Fragile as epiphytes,
tight as silk saris or orange peels:
the truth always gives way.

The day we met
I convinced you I overcame
childhood rickets. Later:
that I flew with John Denver
the night before he died.

Here's a fact:
95% of baby fowl
purchased each Easter
never make it to their first birthday.

Forgive all of this confessing --

but when I told you
if it gets bad
to think of baby ducks
I didn't love you. Not like this.

Prompt:
Like Evans, write a poem in the first person, where the speaker confesses lies
or exaggerations to a "you" -- named or unnamed. Try to include an interesting
twist at the end, as well.

Madeleine Barnes
from *You Do Not Have to Be Good* (2020)

Night Work

My father held a tiny piece of glass
that glittered in his hand
as we walked out into night
into the company of hills
and shambling sheep,
boots pressed against thistledown
and when we were two hours away
from the eclipse, he held the lens
in front of my eyes and I saw
another thing, the bigger thing.
I was afraid and shut my eyes.
The muscles around my heart
tightened as we walked
toward the end of comprehension
exchanging light waves
in silence. It will happen again
in twenty years, he said.
Cautious, coordinating,
Things you know by sight.
Things you know without.

Prompt:
Write a poem about an eclipse, a constellation, or other celestial event or cycle;
include a character (real or imagined) who experiences the event with you.

Jennifer Manthey
from *The Fight* (2023)

Yard-Work, After You Stormed Out of the House

It's spring: the air feels luxurious then cold,

like our bed without you in it.

The gate latch is broken again.

The lawn is greening up. Blades blur like years viewed from a distance.

In the shaded corners, snow melts slow.

I rake carefully -- last year you found a nest of baby rabbits, shallow hole in the middle of the yard.

You guided the lawnmower around it for weeks, let them grow their ears and strong legs peacefully.

I want you to be happy.

Birds trill in the trees.

The sun collapses behind the neighbor's garage.

I've trusted you with everything.

Prompt:
Like Manthey, write a poem consisting of internal dialogue, but written in first person to a person with which the speaker has had an argument or disagreement. Experiment with the idea of short, end-stopped lines, as well as longer lines written in prose-poem format.

Matt Mauch
from *If You're Lucky is a Theory of Mine* (2013)

The ribs and sternum being no kind of fence

I'm going to take my jacket off, let my heart see the leaping fishes
and standing bears that emerge from a tree trunk

once a chainsaw's taken to it.

Pepper-shaped, my heart itches like a wound
just sealed, just beginning to heal.

Having exposed it, I suppose the sun will purple it
so it never blends in.

Why not use a gnat as the thing that best describes
my ability to keep my heart in my chest, off my sleeve,

as in, I have the self-control of a gnat.

A spider my size could carry a house on its shoulders
if it had them.

but gnats and spiders and hearts only grow to be our size in movies
with bloody beginnings, middles, ends.

My heart was a hand. It became a fist.
The story I like to tell

is it closed around a star.

Prompt:
Think of a fable or a story you could tell about your heart, as Mauch does in the
last three lines of the poem. Then write a poem incorporating several metaphors
and images not usually associated with hearts or love.

Lena Khalaf Tuffaha
from *Kaan and Her Sisters*

Miss Sahar Listens to Fairuz Sing "Take Me"

Take me to a house with no doors.
Let the wind carry us, Habibi,
to a country of windows framing the waves,
and leave me on the balcony of the sea.

Let the wind carry us, Habibi,
return us to the days we lived there,
in our country of windows framing the waves,
before our loves departed without farewells.

Return us to the days we lived there,
to a mawaal in the orchard,
before our loves departed without farewells
to wait in the kingdom of forgetting.

Mawaal in the orchard,
lemon blossoms falling from fingers,
I wait for you in the kingdom of forgetting
Habibi, I listen for the echo of your song

and lemon blossoms fall from my fingers.
Take me to a house with no doors,
to a country of windows framing the waves.
I wait for you in the kingdom of forgetting.

Prompt:
Write a poem in a form where lines are repeated - a pantoum, or one which
you invent yourself. Like Tuffaha, choose a topic that is friendly to repetition -
longing, remembrance, or rumination.

Hannah Gamble
from *The Traditional Feel of the Ballroom* (2021)

I Will Explain Infidelity

When you are living in a different part of the country than is your lover,
the one who is right there, and wants you,
is the best one.

Whenever people are surprised that so-and-so has cheated
on a very good-looking person

with a much less good-looking person
I think, You don't know how cheating works.

When I wanted a vacation, the whole point was to go
somewhere different, not better.

And when I wanted to hurt one of the small animals
on my father's property I didn't look for the cutest animal.
In fact, when I found an animal that no one else
was paying attention to, I thought my prospective actions less heinous.

I was only broadening a crack
in an already cracked thing,
like choosing the flattened candy bar to steal.

Prompt:
Write a poem beginning with these lines from Hannah Gamble's poem, exploring
your own experiences or thoughts on her assertion in the poem:

When I wanted a vacation, the whole point was to go
somewhere different, not better.

Iris Jamahl Dunkle
from *Interrupted Geographies* (2017)

Things Given Away

A sharp tongue, clear mind,
sound of hawks circling; life
strung between two pines,

instruction of flight;
salty promise of fog;; first
garden of kale and

red onions nuzzled
by deer; dirt road, the dusty
wash toward impasse; sound

of the far off creek
howling after a hard rain;
a quieted tongue;

a place that washes
away with each passing rain.

Prompt:
Write a poem about things that you've given away -- or perhaps things that
seemed like losses at first, but ended up being worth losing. Notice how Dunkle
uses semicolons and other punctuation in the poem, and experiment with
shorter lines and the use of different punctuation.

Pamela Johnson Parker
from *Cleave* (2017)

The Sixties: Age 10, What I Wanted Was

my name to be poppy and not pamela;
      wanted a mouth that wet, and a paper mini
dress and an Indian gauze skirt crinkly
      as those petals; wanted a flop-brim hat and
go-go boots of white leather, I wanted
      eyeliner and a black velvet choker,
a mary quant flower; a wiglet and lace
      stockings; wanted baby-doll pajamas;
wanted to be thin as a sleeve, straight as
      a twig; wanted tabs for all my clothes; nights
I wanted to be tucked inside a flap,
      filed in a folder, flat as a flitter;
wanted straight hair so I ironed it,
      wanted a flat chest; breasts sprouted anyway.

Prompt:
Make a list of things you wanted when you were a tween - maybe even age 10 -
and use the list to craft a poem. Have some fun experimenting with indented or
staggered lines - how do they affect the poem's flow and tone?

David Groff
from *Live in Suspense* (2023)

Suspense

At last I have learned to shut up.
You squint, pause, shiver,
seized by silence,
in New York a negative soliloquy.

I've grown into the sense
not to tender chatter,
not to let panic preside,
to reside inside myself,

and let our absence be presence.
Still, your eclipse of sound
darkens our table. I know
once you speak, we change.

What secret will your share?
By not asking, do I betray you?
Will love or death, large or small,
rise like a sun or a beast?

This restaurant is wrestling voices,
This espresso is getting cold.
I listen to your eyes.
I live in suspense.

Prompt:
Think about the many words that are related to the word "suspense" but are not
direct synonyms: anticipation; dread; hope; expectation; apprehension. Write a
poem about the experience of waiting from one of these perspectives.

Gabriella R Tallmadge
from *Sweet Beast*

Announcement

My name, from its male origins, meant messenger.

When I said You ruined me, I wanted to reverse the word order,
twin the pain and dig it in you.

The angel Gabriel stood two bows-lengths from a prophet,
craved closeness but, by nature, chose instead his secrets.

You once called me barrier fire, a barrage. As if looking
in the mirror, I am onslaught. A landslide coming closer.

He was meant to be a comfort to a man as he was felled.
Gabriel translated what the earth said, once broken open:

This is in you.

Two by two, we're both no good. We are
the other's flood sentence.

This is done, said Gabriel. And this is the new.

Prompt:
Look up the meaning of your name, and use it to generate a poem in which you
personify the meaning of your name in an interaction with another person. Like
Tallmadge, be willing to make leaps and/or construct stanzas that are loosely
connected.

Artress Bethany White
from *My Afmerica* (2019)

Abecedarian for Peace

Accept that I have penned another elegy.
Besieged, the dead occupy my brain.
Comfort reigns in words on a page, a
Descant to lift the pain.
Etched into memory are names, a
Flood of American blood.
Grasping each day like a lifeline, I beg
Humanity to realign and
Inspire the gun to empty,
Just not into another body.

Kindred, I say consider peace.
Lofty goals can birth kindness in times of crisis.
Meet eyes to pass the love,
Not the hate that elongates days.
Opine carefully and
Perform lead, not bit parts. Pause before
Questioning civil rights, and I might not
Retaliate with a litany to halt a
Shrug at another lost life.
Trudge through history and stumble
Upon reflection. Pause to name the fallen.
Validate the battlefield and let
Wisdom decry the damage done. Come, explore this
Xyst of the mind with me; a garden holding the day's tally.
Yowl a refusal to wall our brethren and hear the
Zither play while we mend the broken.

Prompt:
Write an Abecedarian poem in the second person point of view, as White has
done, in which you exhort, ask, and/or tell the "you" to act.

Iris Jamahl Dunkle
from *Gold Passage* (2013)

Bobcat

Here on my doorstep,
cricket song and frog swell.
By now, the bobcat
I'd spotted in the front yard
is deep in the woods--
his freedom full and risen as a moon.

My matter is never freed
from urban tongue and lure.
I pace my house, plot escape,
jump at whistles of tea kettles,
the screams of time's alarms
while the bobcat freely looms
in memory. Overhead,
planes fly courses, leave
long contrails that linger,
dissolve, but stay.

Prompt:
Write a poem about encountering a wild animal in an unexpected place (this
can be an actual encounter or a fictional encounter). Explore the boundaries
between the wilderness and "civilization" in your poem.

Christian Gullette
from *Coachella Elegy* (2024)

Gadolinium (Gd)

Intravenous ions,
metallic complex for the MRI scan,

I watch his body become an interstate
of dye-drenched veins,

contrast agent tracing
the melanoma gripping the back of his eye.

Whatever privacies there are in this body,
they are different than what he arrived with,

a body happening as I watch it,
microscopic spaces now paramagnetic,

coursing with gadolinium, one of the rare-earths
though I'm barely acquainted with the world

blurring before me. I pretend to understand these scans.
His brain looks like water

after rinsing a brush or a night view from space,
the planet's cities

phosphorescing grids
where darkness adheres to the edges.

Prompt:
Write a poem about a medical test or procedure you or a loved one has
experienced. Include some information/scientific details, but also explore
metaphors and imagery.

Susan L Leary
from *Dressing the Bear* (2024)

The Professor Asks Me to Write a Joyful Poem

One without drugs or sadness
or mention of your death. One
in which you don't beat your fists
bloody against a palm. I am
disobedient as is joy as is you,
as is the better version of the truth
that lives inside the defense. Is it more
profound to say walking towards
or walking away? Somehow, with me,
you're always doing both: forgetting
the air mattress & your Greyhound
ticket, then forgetting to breathe.
Is forgetfulness a form of joy
or of disobedience? The day I forgot
the plunger at Ace Hardware
was the day you forgot
to put my car in park. You were fifteen,
so my fault, but as the car rolled
nearer the storefront, we laughed
through the panic because joy is you
is disobedience is me, is the weather
we last looked upon your face.
A shit storm, you'd have said,
as we ran out to the parking lot, pelted
by the sky's sadness & with nothing
for a shield, while I was thinking
how nice it would have been
to spend a day with you in the rain.

Prompt:
Most of us who write poetry have had the (usually unpleasant) experience of
having someone tell us what we should (or shouldn't) write a poem about. Like
Leary, try your hand at starting a poem with a line indicating who has told you
want to write or not write about, and see what kind of poem develops.

Pamela Johnson Parker
from *Cleave* (2018)

Something to Declare

Documentary: The thick flat brushes,
The glass of water gone grey with color,
the rough white paper, then your deft salvage
Of the smudges I'd made; how you told me
About accident, about chance and balance;
How you bit your lip as you worked; how quickly
We went to bed. Like air, you said. You can
Never get enough. Later, you painted
Me in oils, the fluorescent lights leaching
The color from my skin, my mouth a gash
Of Persian red--and after you're gone, I couldn't
Bear to sell it. In my garage now, it's stored
Beside that pair of Japanese herons:
Red-capped, stilted, the ones that mate for life.

Prompt:
Write about a personal gift or memento you've kept, even though the person
who gave it to you has passed away or the relationship has ended. Why do you
hold on to it? Do you keep it a secret that you still have the item, or do you
display it?

Issam Zineh
from *Unceded Land* (2022)

Swipe Left to View the Same Image in Visible Light
after Jenny Molberg

there is a fine line between looking and not looking
even finer still the thing said and left unsaid
there's an expression in Arabic that translates to either shoot him
or break his brain the closest equivalent to a bull in a china shop
with room for interpretation as there might be between, say, presence and
embodiment
the original expression used to go god is in the details
avoidance can look something like intention from the outside
my therapist says liberation comes from writing down the details
in one context what is expected in another means a public death
how willing we must have been to take that chance
take for instance what will become of that bowl of fruit you leave out overnight
take for instance what came before you that you forgot you inherited
take for instance what came of an imagined wolf whistle
take for instance what became of that girl who lost a tooth in her dad's knuckle
take for instance what might come from a mistimed recollection
take for one final instance what might come from a split second of noticing
the gaze in its violent shimmering--a knife in the grass--

Prompt:
Begin a poem with a phrase in another language, and its literal translation into
English, as Zineh does - and explore the meanings behind the phrases as you
allow the poem to unfurl.

Steven Riel
from *Fellow Odd Fellow* (2013)

excerpt from **The Teacup I Desire**

The pattern of teacup I desire
depicts bouquets of mauve roses
tied together by just-picked violets.
Once tea's poured out, a sipping
striptease could reveal thorn
by thorn, as Earl Grey eases
down the length of stem,
at last unveiling unopened buds,
their inviting scents
glazed beneath sugar sediments.

To lift this flowery
vessel in my hands,
to walk it to the cashier, & blushing
or not, to state, I'd like this,
would draw a noticeable dot
out where it could be
connected.

Prompt:
Write about a little luxury item you have always wanted - describe it in detail,
but also how you imagine you would treat the item, use the item, etc. How
would owning the item change your definition of yourself, or how you imagine
other people would see you?

Artress Bethany White
from *My Afmerica*

The Race

We are the only black family in the subdivision,
and your family is the poorest. This is not a matter
of bank accounts, which we know nothing about,
but the pea-green concrete of your house
prefaced by a yard more bald than hirsute.
In an enclave of Spanish-style villas and Tudors
you stand out like the soiled bare feet
and fringe of your teenage brother's cut-off shorts.
The way he fumes, when I best him
in a road race at half his age, leaves me to consider
if it was my years or color that offended him most.
Friendship between us is as amorphous
as me never meeting your parents,
yet not defining you by the ticks we delicately pluck
from your dog's back and smash beneath rocks,
while I wonder if my parents would notice
a pilfered flea collar from our own Hartz three-pack.

Prompt:
Write a narrative poem about an experience from your childhood with a friend
who differed from you in race, income, or another way. As White does, include
your own interpretations of the experience, both at the time of the experience
and now.

Kirk Wilson
from *Songbox*

Quarantine

Poison to each other
we watch the same

murder scenes
not again but again

the roads of voices
the histories

we hold underwater
wave on wave

the next echoing
the first exactly

What ancient
time has now become

the cities fortified
against a siege

the walls come down
again the air behind

the air tastes close
again like anything

is possible
and this time

everything could happen
just a little differently.

Prompt:
Try writing a poem with very short lines, in which you explore your own
experiences during the COVID-19 pandemic with isolation, sheltering in place,
and/or quarantine.

Darren Demaree
from *Two Towns Over* (2018)

You Can Do Anything in the Walmart as Long as You Don't Touch the Bicycles

House of my belonging,
I wore a dirty dress
& empty Coke twelve-packs

as shoes, I ate marshmallows
straight from the bag
& changed all of the televisions

to a Thursday football game
& I definitely remember
peeing in a children's potty

& everything was rosy
until I unhooked one bike
& proved myself

to be an undeniable victor
in a short race that ended
near the bulk t-shirt aisle.

Prompt:
Write a humorous persona poem about misbehaving in public. If you need inspiration, try looking at "News of the Weird" or other online sources.

Notes

Page 7. Issam Zoneh's *Citrine* modifies a line from Sinan Antoon's *The Book of Collateral Damage* translated by Jonathan Wright (Yale University Press, 2019).

Page 26. Issam Zoneh's *Swipe Left to View the Same Image in Visible Light*: The poem's title comes from a NASA Instagram post in which two Hubble telescope images of the Eagle Nebula's Pillars of Creation are shown side by side (one in infrared and one in visible light). The Poem's first and last lines are after Jenny Molberg's "Epistle from the Funambulist Hospital for Invisibility " (from *Refusal*, LSU Press, 2020).

Author Index

About This Book

Since its founding in 2012, Trio House Press has published more than 35 books of poetry through both its contests, The Trio Award and Louise Bogan Award, and through editorial selections. We are privileged to have had the opportunity to publish these poets and are pleased to be sharing their work with you, along with some prompts that you can use to generate work of your own. All proceeds from this book go towards production costs for future books. Thank you for supporting Trio House Press in its mission to bring new and exciting voices into American poetry.

Find out more about Trio House Press and current titles by visiting our website: www.triohousepress.org

Printed in the USA
CPSIA information can be obtained
at www.ICGtesting.com
CBHW030719010424
6155CB00004B/9